Mountain Travel

Dona Herweck Rice

Publishing Credits

Rachelle Cracchiolo, M.S.Ed., *Publisher*
Conni Medina, M.A.Ed., *Managing Editor*
Nika Fabienke, Ed.D., *Content Director*
Véronique Bos, *Creative Director*
Shaun N. Bernadou, *Art Director*
Carol Huey-Gatewood, M.A.Ed., *Editor*
John Leach, *Assistant Editor*
Courtney Roberson, *Senior Graphic Designer*

Image Credits: All images from iStock and/or Shutterstock.

Teacher Created Materials
5301 Oceanus Drive
Huntington Beach, CA 92649-1030
www.tcmpub.com

ISBN 978-1-4938-9856-5

Printed in China
Nordica.082018.CA21800936

How do some people

go to the  ?

bottom

They may  .

ski

How do some people

go to the  ?

bottom

They may  .

snowboard

How do some people

go to the  ?

bottom

They may  .

sled

How do some people go to the  ?

bottom

They may  .

ride

How do some people go to the  ?

bottom

They may  .

drive

High-Frequency Words

New Words

do	go
how	may
people	some

Review Words

the	they
to	